Angels & Empty Pages

Angels & Empty Pages

Terry Boyle

THE **BLACK SPRING**
PRESS GROUP

First published in 2023
by The Black Spring Press Group
Maida Vale Publishing imprint
Maida Vale, London W9,
United Kingdom

Typeset and cover design by Edwin Smet

978-1-915406-43-9

*The editor has generally followed American spelling and punctuation
at the author's request.*

BLACKSPRINGPRESSGROUP.COM

To all those who have peopled
my life and left a lasting impression

TABLE OF CONTENTS

STITCHING

You speak to me now of folding time and space
into that moment
when the pieces of our life began,
the pieces of you and me
woven into the fabric of that moment,
which pieced and stitched us together
with the thread that binds one heart to another;
into another moment when time and space
unfolds itself to us,
not as a ticking clock but as a carpet of stars,
brightly twinkling through dark-coloured joy.

THE MARROW OF MY WORDS

I want to walk where no one has gone before,
rub the innocence of my soul deeply
into an uninhabited timeless space;
slather its fullness, until flesh becomes word,
and my destination reads unknown.

I want to pick some unnamed exotic fruit,
gamble my existence on a dangerous beauty,
feel the thrill of breathing scented air,
ripe with virginal thoughts of dark rosebuds,
and throwing soft petals to a careless breeze.

I want to speak to an unknown God
who does not hide among the clouds,
unadorned by ritual and pomp,
whose pain and sorrow are etched
into the marrow of my being.
Together, eating the bread of our tears,
we'll share a cup of friendship and love,
and celebrate the wonder of our imaginings.

LANGUAGE OF ANGELS

For Katie

When I dream, eternity poses itself
as angels kneeling on clouds;
but it's easy for them to look ethereal,
their existence lies outside of time and space.
In these dreams,
language flows out of me in unimaginable ways,
tributaries of speech with no identifiable source,
twisting and turning in immeasurable infinities,
yet, for some reason, these dreams make me sad.

We've been in lockdown forever,
or so it seems,
in a shrinking world that contracts daily,
moments slip from one day to the next,
reducing us to rituals and routines,
our demise, it seems, only a matter of time,
impermanence is the burden of our dis-ease.

In my dream state,
I listen to angels guilelessly singing
their beautiful harmonies, electrifying the air,
resounding in unison, resplendent in tone,
yet alien to this sickly soul of mine,
and, for some reason, their strange music saddens me.

My finite life decreases bit by bit,
minutes, seconds, drag on and on.
Existence wears heavily when survival is threatened.
My neighbours sing to cheer themselves up
until one by one, each voice is silenced.

Still, I listen as those dreamy angels sing to me.
Oblivious to our woes and fears.
They are unearthly as the clouds, and perfectly surreal.

Waking,
my fallen angel wings thrash wildly.
I cannot move.
My body is confined to a narrow chamber,
unintelligible, mechanical noises, grinding,
discordant in tone;
my eyes see only an infinite void of whiteness.
Bellows syphon air into my paralyzed lungs.

A priestly woman approaches,
her face shield intuitively understands
the useless dreams of a trapped angel.

Praying, her words beckon me upwards,
beyond my glass cage,
where angels live without fear of dying.

FLIGHT OF FANCY

I laughed at romance,
scorned those who had succumbed,
not knowing I'd fall to its charm,
not knowing I'd soar into its rapture
gliding playfully among its thermals,
ascending to the very heavens with daring dexterity.

Your smile lights up my heart
as clear as day,
sky blue, alive with glorious chirpings.
We are songbirds, cascading on an invisible
weave of passionate desire.
Crashing downwards, we are exhilarated
until the upward draw catches us in a beautiful dive.

Your springtime call lilts in my ears;
the sound of my name softly cooed
in that secret place, where our souls' nest,
cosseted by cosy gentle laughter,
and the gentle rubs of lovers preening.

ORA PRO NOBIS

My daily visitation with the angel of anxiety
has not gone well.
It seems that I'm not as strong as I thought.
Plagued with the usual arsenal of woes,
predictions of pestilence and disease wiped me out.
Was yesterday's slight cough the rattle of death?

Today, my thoughts appear asymptomatic,
but I could still be a virus spreader.

The mask I'm wearing is for your benefit,
not mine.

Guilt? Yes, guilty as charged.
Paying a surrogate shopper to cross the aisles,
putting them in danger so I can stop worrying,
but I worry now about them crossing into the next life.

This is progress, isn't it? I asked my virus friend.
Nothing.
I find his non-directive approach to my fear maddening.
No, I'm not in denial,
the media has taken care of that.
A 24/7 guessing game of potential harm
is a true mind fuck!
Sure, I'm angry. Ebola, Avian flu, SARS,
signs disregarded prove costly.

Bargaining?
Enough candles for a menorah,
Novenas to delight the famous and not-so-famous,
sufficient prayer flags to bring down the celestial Buddha

himself,
be assured my ecumenism is wholeheartedly sincere.

Yes, I know too much religion is depressing.
No, I cannot accept virtual silence as profound.
I don't care if doctors have some inside track
or the latest news on new mutations.
What I've learned from this pandemic is regret,
for the things I've not said, a life not fully lived,
friendships I've not valued, and how did I ever
underestimate the beauty of my mundane life?

GILEAD

When I grasp the blade, ambiguity bleeds out.
It was the bomb maker who said I was fearfully
and wonderfully made,
so, implode or explode, I will most certainly bleed to death.
If I didn't laugh about my tentative grip on life, I would slip,
fall into the all too recognizable home space.

It's the place where I grew up,
a myriad of barbed brute force realities,

'Can ye box?'

'Naw, I'm a pacifist.'

'Alright then, pass a fist.'

Our family's rite of passage proves if you're a real man.

'You're a sly one Boyle.'

Branded on the first day at secondary school
by a teacher's time-sensitive words served to detonate,
and blast through a lifetime.

On the bedroom door hung my drawing of Jesus,
under constant siege from my brothers' allies,
Connolly, Marx and Tone.
When the messiah's sight was removed with a fag end,
I was left worshipping a blind God.

'Boyle, you're one of them, aren't you?'

The English soldier's accent had a sharp edge to it.

'Your brothers still up to their usual tricks.'

The image of three wise monkeys appeared before me
as I stood there blind, deaf and dumb.

PTSD, it's the new way to explain the unexplainable.

'Your brain can only tolerate so much.
It's wonderful how the mind copes with fear.'
The therapist's words dipped in saccharine solutions,
brought no relief.

'Let go of the blade, let the blood dry and heal,
find your way back to a newly created reality,
soothing a troubled soul.'

Emerging, clutching the scars of my wounds,
I cried, 'Is there no balm in Gilead?'

RED BOW TIED

I removed your handsome green shirt
from a closet full of memories.
Neatly folded, lying benignly on the bed,
waiting to be bagged, destination undetermined,
soon to be zipped up into its black plastic soul.

A charity shop is a noble and virtuous choice,
your mantle resting on the shoulders of a man
your stature.
After all, it's only fair that your vibrancy
be given another chance to rejuvenate.

Empty spaces stagnate my weeping hours,
knowingly, they stare blankly back at me,
indifferent to my pain, to my loss.
They surround my every thought with
your absence.

Ubiquitous black bags, tied in a pretty red bow,
hide my painful memories from sight;
a sunflower silhouetted by the evening sun,
captured in a rare hourglass moment;
somewhere in France
your laughing green shirt sipping on the *joie de vivre*
from a near-empty glass.
Now, they're neatly tied and bound, sealed in black,
hidden from life.

Misshapen black bulks are stuffed in the boot of the car;
my world, and a thousand shared lifetimes, bagged,
their destination unknown.

A rubbish tip is a less noble choice,
rats gnawing out the heart of my heart,
tearing our universe into a million pieces,
while I remain weeping among empty spaces,
prolonging my vigil into
a fourth, fifth day and no stone unturned.

A SMITHY FOR THE POPULACE

'Poetry's hot these days', he said,
people, hooked on a lexicon of adjectives
can be very addictive.
Notes of far-flung fancy and hype inspire,
keep them buzzed.
Put more action into those meandering ideas,
and you'll be smoking hot too.

Lights, action, thesaurus!

They'll love you when your metaphors sing,
it's a rap.
Train those words to wink, not think, smile, not frown,
and for God's sake sex up your vocabulary.

Fire up those words with world-changing ideas,
avoid complexity, regress to small bytes,
strike while the words are still sizzling,
it's cool.
Let the rush of verbosity course through you.
Set all those superfluous puns on the run;
slang and vernacular are marketable these days,
so, keep stock of your exchanges.

Am I a mere hawker of words?
Scheming rhymes into a haze of frenzy,
just for the novelty of it,
selling them off with a well-paid kiss?

I love the shadows of words,
the mysterious nuances that fall into strange forms,
and the abstractions born from the mystery of being.

The beautiful wonders of language, the stuff of art.

'Poetry's hot these days', he said,
then why does it all seem so hollow?

SIX FEET APART

We covered our faces in fear
and our hearts opened,
we kept ourselves a grave apart,
six feet to remind us of what we fear.
Connected now by virtual intimacy
we brave the isolation,
our hands, hidden from touch,
reach out to a host of solitary souls,
ritually washing, cleansing the flesh,
all of us grieving the loss of fellowship,
as we wait for the day until we have faces.

SEASONED TO TASTE

After my retirement, to be taken with a pinch of salt

The crumb, that is my soul, is often bland,
insipid, and lacks something.
I've tried giving it to God but *He* declined the offer,
maybe the basic ingredient, that's me, falls short.
Am I too rich to the taste, or too bitter?
Expressionless, looking away, *He* leaves me to guess
as to why *He's* wholly indifferent?
Or maybe *He's* used to the Good stuff?

Satan often stops by and asks if he might
season me to taste,
but his schmaltzy manner offends my pride,
as does his love of the hot and spicy,
a bit too rich for my Irish constitution.
It constantly annoys me that his ADHD makes it
impossible for me to keep his attention;
with him, I cannot avoid the creeping reality that
my soul is not one of a kind,
certainly, not one of his kind.

The world passes me without a second glance.
I am no longer freshly baked,
there's not a whiff of yeastiness left in me,
I'm stale, grown hard, and crusty,
with the essential goodness bleached out of my soul,
by the acrid airs of academia.
So, with no takers, I'm forced to
contemplate the fate of a well-seasoned crumb.

THINGS I'VE LEFT BEHIND

Many have taken this road,
some when it was much less travelled
but that was a long time ago,
and we've heard their stories,
stories about travellers who never return.

Nowadays, everyone travels,
packing up their summer or winter gear,
they discover the big world for a week or two,
always returning to real life.

Dipping their toes into a new place,
they sample its fare like newbie adventurers
but all the while knowing it's for fun,
a respite from the usual mundane rituals of home.

But not for me,
I look at things now with a grieving sigh,
touch familiar objects with a deep longing.
I know that this trip will be different,
the plane ticket has a fake return date,
costs are cheaper that way,
it's the real cost of my one-way departure
that remains unimaginable.

STARS IN THEIR EYES

My mother unknowingly gave birth to chaos,
breastfeeding me to the tune of social disparity.
I grew up among those who had enough;
enough of believing in the lie,
a rich lie to convince the poor that they
were wrong in wanting more,
more of what everyone should rightfully have.

Disorganized, and constantly out of sorts,
I grew up out of step with my generation,
feeling different, when difference wasn't cool
in Derry City; the town I still don't love so well,
but liked it well enough to use it, placing me
inside and outside its boundaries.

Leaving Ireland wasn't easy despite my ambivalence.
I aimed to own the world and claim it as my own
until my hopes rested heavily on the American Dream.

Now Mother Liberty amuses and confuses me;
satirizing herself with every empty platitude,
birthing me daily into a host of chaotic delusions.
I travel now through the insularity of white privilege,
walking a line bordering a nation's madness
of godly heights immortalized in a slavish past,
with muscle-bound dreams and enough stripes
to dominate the very stars.

THE WONDER OF RENEWAL

Under these sheets, love plays amorously,
hidden from a prying sun.
Under these sheets,
the bright splendour of my tears
illuminates in your generous heart,
so ready, so fully alive, it vibrantly
ousts the shadows of my fears.
Under these sheets,
I venerate your soul's gentle light,
with naked expectancy.

Beneath these sheets,
there are no hackneyed phrases;
words are born anew on your tongue,
remaking worlds, healing old wounds,
so that my anxious thoughts find rest
in lullaby eyes that calm my restlessness.
Beneath these sheets,
I fall into the quiet arms of silent repose.

HOLY OF HOLIES

I walked with angels before I knew you,
their harps playing deftly to a broken chord.
I shaved my head, and opened my heart to them,
touching their feet with true devotion,
but they only wept to hear my wilderness song
and my constant longing for a new kind of music.

Shades courted me before you came,
ghosting the radiant courtyard of my heart,
refusing to enter into the Holy of Holies
where I, and I alone passionately knew
I was out of harmony with the universe,
treading on a starry path in search of a sign,
waking, sleeping, finding day and night
friendless, until the day you came.

Your laughter flickers now in this holy temple,
scattering darkness into ghostly flight.
You sing to me a sanctified song of flesh and blood,
preparing a way for your sacred love to rest
on the breast of a devoted one.
It was that day when heaven fell from my eyes
and I saw you, a man among the gods.

CLOUD OF CONTENTMENT

Words, felled in trees, are fast disappearing,
it's the click-and-mouse games that are the new thing.
Heaven has been sublet to help with rising costs,
the man above is to introduce a new marketing scheme;
angels and archangels must put their collective wings
together and create a more user-friendly environment.
A new economy, with less pomposity and ceremony,
will become a virtual revelation of multimedia glory.

Connectivity, composed of interpersonal relations,
will be phased out in favour of less risky behaviours.
Platforms, created for brief encounters, prove popular
if you don't mind the gap.
Human interaction is to be contained, and minimized;
in the new economy, health and survival are paramount
and require us to curb the urge to merge.

Plagues are a small price to pay for progress,
hosting demons, due to our curious interactions.
Thankfully, now in sterile spaces, we explore a web
of our own making.
The new economy ensures such conveniences are satisfying,
on a cloud of contentment, we will live out our existence,
heavenly mansions apportioned to us in mega, giga,
tera, and petabytes,
a mystical place to upload your soul to the great matrix
where you can ascend and descend in lucid dreams,
but, for now, let not your hearts be troubled,
it's all about to change.

WHAT'S IN A PIECE OF EARTH?

What's in a piece of earth?
People, none of them ready to die;
we cannot see them nor where they lie.
What's in a piece of earth?
Lives short-lived, rich love forever lost;
in Treblinka, the dark soul of the Holocaust.
What's in a piece of earth?
A bloody field of buried unquiet dreams,
with no ladder to the sky, no divine schemes.
What's in a piece of earth?
Fathers, mothers, and children all huddled there,
smothering, rotting in their despair.
What's in a piece of earth?
Grasses, flowers brimming to burst,
all silent now…
What's in a piece of earth?
The best and the worst of us.

SATISFIED HEART

I crave more time with you.
Time to devour, strip bare each moment,
with not one second unaccounted for,
conscious only of the eye of Chronos
jealously watching us
tear and devour each segment,
savouring the forbidden fruit of each hour
stolen from the lap of the gods.

My love for you spans an infinity,
minute by minute, its unending beginning
stretches eagerly out of a satisfied heart.
Inching towards the unrevealed vista of you,
I traverse the timeless garden of your soul
marvelling at your wonderful abundance,
ripening, indulging myself in the succulent juices,
relishing each glorious morsel that brings you to me.

HERE'S TO BEING THRAN!

As a child, I was strong-willed,
they told me I had backbone.
My rebellious nature was enjoyed,
it was even considered cute,
back then.

A thran teenager is never easy,
bolshie, determined to be right.
'It's a phase he's going through,
he'll grow out of it soon enough,'
they said.

I can't help it,
digging myself into a shallow grave,
the cute factor has long since died away,
a passing phase, now a lifelong trait,
of a stubborn, stiff-necked, old man,
they say.

But what isn't said or seen,
is my thranness is a charm.
It wards off the inner critic
and fuels me with determination and grit.
This child has grown up to be strong enough
to embrace his contradictions
because I'm thran.

*'Thran' in Ireland means stubborn. It originates from the German language,
although the original meaning is lost to us.*

CUT TO THE BONE

I dare not speak of who I am,
the shades of me that elude you
who see things so definitively,
crudely drawn in outline;
you, who are blind to the nod-and-wink
of mischievous tautology,
deaf to my curtsied nuances,
you, who only listen to the blade-cutting
sound of bone,
fleshed open by blunted words.

MY DARK MUSE

Amid the darkness, I sweat tears of sorrow.
Stale air fills my lagging lungs,
whose pistons indolently rise
and fall during my laboured musings,
where nothing new or good is created
only the suffocation blackness of night spreading outwards.

I hack a discordant melodious jingle,
consumptively sterile in rhyme,
its cadence expectorated in futility,
I find nothing virtuous with this dark muse.

Eventide curdles my thoughts to a thick sludge,
asphyxiates me with its fading sublimity.
Stars wink sardonically at me,
emptying the sky of simile and metaphor,
until nothing is left but a polished stainless-steel moon.

I long for daylight, to hear my song in Excelsis,
and the soaring flight of an untethered mind,
gliding among the currents of an unformed lyric,
swooping gloriously low in wonderful adjectives,
released in meter, wooed by a flirtatious sun,
I rhythmically ascend to a sensuous air,
plucked on the harp of Beauty herself.

But the night will come again,
shapes and colours will scurry off once more
to hide behind this wall of silence.
Beauty will blindly flounder,
grieving her wholeness, harmony and radiance,
her tender music will die in the night's empty embrace,
leaving me to choke in its deathly silence.

DIVINE SCRABBLE

I'm all fingers and thumbs.
Predictively, words appear from nothing,
refusing to comply with my wishes.
I will drop them into the well of good luck,
even if my luck isn't that good.

He spoke with flawless eloquence
every word performed perfectly,
so, I reconstructed his message
changed it into a wild beast of a thing,
left it to create its unique meaning.

I should know better,
an empty well isn't a sign of good luck.

'Prayers are perfect for you', he said,
'Order your thoughts into Godly words',
but my texts refuse to offer homage,
they lustily rebel against the moral objective,
scrabbling through a riotous lexicon,
to become resurrected in glorious disorder.

My thumb proves hopeless for texting,
too many embarrassing typos,
that casually throw me under the bus
and rob me of all common decency,
reconstructing my intention without rhyme,
and leaving me devoid of all reason.

Tonight, I pillow my tired thoughts of you
that neither finds respite nor refuge from
the restless pilgrim
who tirelessly seeks you out
among the stars.

Resting

Lying on the soft breast of yesterday,
satisfied with pleasant recreations,
I recall the delightful sacred trysts,
content with the desire that creeps
between the sheets of my recollections.

Dreaming

Anarchy plucks the heart of my imagination,
orchestrating new terrors,
fearful wanderings, things lost or forgotten,
people lost but not forgotten.
Among the dross of everyday experience
my vagrant soul lies
crippled by each new ghoulish configuration.

Awake

Gently, the heat of day returns me
to my pillow, cold, clammy to the touch.
Slowly, I wake to a noisy alarm
asserting the order of things,
pandemonium reluctantly relinquishes its hold,
as I recall the wanderings of my unruly soul
when joy is restored by your three heart-shaped emojis.

FOOTNOTES

England will always be a footnote to my life,
always interrupting the flow.
I'm not an IRA sort of person, far from it,
but Britannia is written on almost every page
and more than a reference point for additional
information.

Language ebbs out of me in remote waves,
well-learned ripples making perfect sense.
Listening to native Irish speakers seems foreign,
their ripples make no sense to me.
We look, act, and think the same,
but our thoughts pour into a different sea.

But when Mise Éire plucks at her harp strings,
together, we rise on the crest of a lingering lamentation,
held by a melodious melancholy,
like a fine mizzle on a foggy past,
foolishly, trying to cover up the naked ache,
transporting myself to a time before footnotes.

THE MYTH OF ONE

Who said that there can only be one?
One person to make you wholly one.
When two become one,
someone's light is diminished,
and we lose sight of who we are.
Love is blind.

There's no one true faith to guide us,
no singular source, God indivisible,
divides and conquers all of us,
buries us under a just true cause
that is hopelessly one-sided.

One faith, one God, one people,
Cycloptic, singularly one-dimensional,
monoliths created in drab metaphysics,
blind to curiosity, monosyllabic,
without a single doubt in its veracity.

Many are the ways to understand,
for when a heart is open to the many,
we are nourished by a love of contradiction.

Doubt the absolute truth of everything,
and then you can unmask the myth of oneness.

ODE TO A CLOTHES LINE

By the rivers of Babylon, we sat down and wept

— Psalm 137

Pegged with the usual icons of ordinariness,
a washing line blusters in a midsummer's breeze
to distract me from my religious duties.

Entranced by the cosmic playfulness
of clothes wildly dancing in the wind,
mesmerizingly chaotic,
my heart beats to their silent music,
nullifying the empty rituals of penance.

Colours rising, gusting in transcendence,
gracelessly, seductive in their tempestuous ease.

A common line of everyday happenings
carries me to a place of beatific joy,
far from that which leashes my song to solemnity.

Inside, the room begins to feel smaller,
a solid and immutable voice booms out,
stringently fervorous in its lack of appeal,
striking my epiphanies with the force of a boot,
cursing the air with the ravings of a vengeful God
demanding my attention while its kick is
aimed at the face of my wandering curiosity.

For a moment, I resist this call to order,
my gaze shifting back to the jubilant sway
of non-conformity —

a child's uninhibited short trousers
jauntily toss to and fro, unrestrained,

a white bra brazenly flashes in the sun,
boldly teasing, strikingly defiant,
a shirt ripples out in brute strength,
gloriously vigorous and virile.

Still, the righteous heel continues to strike out
against this fragile reverie of ordinariness,
truncating its beauty with unimagined catastrophes,
separating me with the savage breath of God,
muting its freedom song with medieval strangeness.

GLORIA IN EXCELSIS DEO

For so long we were out there,
now in here we're safe from out there.
Once the world was getting smaller and smaller,
now it's bigger, more distant, and isolated.
Once we worried about our carbon footprint,
but now our footprints are silently being erased.
Global warming, radical environmental changes
were once the big issues,
now they're replaced by a simple microbe.

A virus has changed what we thought we knew.
It stood at the door and knocked.
At first, we ignored its profound presence,
failed to understand its true significance,
until we found ourselves evicted.
Once we raised our faces to kiss the face of God
but now our prayers have become a feeble cough.

BLIND SOUL

My ocean heart delights in the cresting of the waves,
dolphins sing out to me, harmonizing with verbose whales.
Mermaids intrigue me, charming foolish sailors
into risking their comfort for an icy embrace.
Tempestuous, indifferent yet sustaining life,
eulogized in verse, my turbulence is beyond language,
my volatility not tethered to any immutable force.
Unbridled white horses course through
this oceanic heart of the world,
                    for I am anarchy,
the unrestrained blind soul of natural contradiction.

ELEGY TO FREEDOM

Lost at sea, the American Dream

The Hudson rushes below Lady Liberty's feet,
a surge of impermanency passing beneath her gaze.
Her mausoleum heart, calcified by apathy,
stoically watches over this safe harbour,
her unwashed feet shackled to a popular lie.

Around her crown, a cloud of witnesses gathers,
ghostly voices echoing in unison a cautionary note,
warnings of treachery drowned out by the throng
of would-be believers, desperate men and women,
dreamers, following in the wake of beautiful ideas,
all of them doomed to be wrecked on her shores.

I have watched and wondered where freedom truly lies.
We, who were once lost at sea, searching for a home,
wistfully vulnerable to Lady Liberty's solicitations.
Our ears, pricking up at the mere whisper of hope,
spellbound by hope, and her calls for liberation,
echoed in rousing anthems, and cosmetic optimism,
inviting us to forfeit our dreams and become flotsam.

BIG MAN

He was never an idle man, a Paddy
among Paddies on England's roadways,
this small wiry man who eclipses me still,
paving his way into my troubled thoughts
with brusque muscular masculinity,
digging into the heart and soul of me.

A Dickensian Donegal childhood was his,
rural Ireland creates another scrapper,
blighted with rickets and deprivation,
starved of literacy, incapable of walking,
he found his fists before he found his feet.

Derry's big smoke looked down on his ways,
cornering him in all his subsequent choices,
squaring up to him to come out fighting.
My mother spoon-fed him a paltry education,
paving the way for him to write bookie slips
and sign the dole, as one of Derry's own.

Drinking made the world dwarf around him,
his fists grew bigger than Finn McCool's.
Sporting bruises like a proud Neanderthal,
shouting commands to us in garbled Irish,
his whole brutish charade abhorrent to me.

Traversing through three degrees in English,
I polished my speech with the Queen's tongue,
trimmed all my wee giveaway idiosyncrasies,
enunciating each syllable with deliberation,
driven to be the polar opposite of a Paddy
but doffing my cap in unnecessary gratitude.

My mind, intoxicated with drams of knowledge,
imbibed shot after shot of gigantic ideas,
designed to diminish his stature, to surpass
the mangled speech of my youth and prove
I'd finally outgrown his oafish myopic ways.

Sobering up, he got leaner and much smaller.
No longer feeding his archaic macho ego
his true self emerged, sensitive, big-hearted.
Tirelessly, labouring to be a lesser man
he became an even greater human being.
The big man who lives inside my head.

Shedding bluster and wrath for compassion,
he found his feet when he started paving
the road for other big men and women
journeying towards their true greatness.

When cancer began to devour him,
we knew that what was coming after
was bigger than any of us, bigger than life itself,
the giant that takes all we have in its grip,
and gives nothing back.
He fought mightily against that Colossus,
and lost,
the real man whose raging compassion
and big heart still eclipse me to this day.

FIRESTARTER

Time fiddles as our hearts burn.
Merrily dancing within the flames of love,
we relish its soft embraces, all of me in you,
smouldering in the embers that carry us towards
the gentle stirrings of a morning breeze,
where love fades to a whispering wisp of joy.

Love, they say, hurts when it heals,
heals as it hurts, disassembles the known,
licks our souls clean with its fiery kisses,
consumes our bodies in a torrid maelstrom.
Love unifies you in me, and the me in you,
its infinite passion beating within the breast of eternity,
where our spirits fade to an infinite joyful whisper.

STAND-ALONE HOUSE

After reading Silkin's poem 'Death of a Son'

Literary bricks and mortar prove no escape
from the silent thing that slumps into your art,
there is no gentle release to be had in a poem.

He is the memory stone your heart refuses to drop,
reverberating heavily in every brick-ish word,
refusing to be subdued by symbol and literary affectation.
Born of his loneliness, your grief stares
at us through an empty window, speechless.

In abstraction, I walk with you on your daily path,
wondering how deep the sadness goes,
the cavernous ache you bear, before it becomes
bricked up in a poem.

There is no end to your stolid metaphors,
no words to aid the silent torture of being
alone.
Forced to face his final quietude,
you are determined to make the calm restless,
as you attempt to take blood from a word.

Even after all these years, it feels raw to me,
his muteness, singing out in your detached observation,
the nameless child's suffering whom you
mummified in verse.

WINGS OF A DOVE

Someone pushed the button, pulled the switch,
opened the gates of hell, and the deluge came.
At first, we refused to believe the changing narratives,
until the outbreak ripped through our bodies,
blindly attacking our misconceptions.
Immune to all our defences,
millions died when the deadly assassin moved in.

Go forth and multiply

A giant storm came at us, knocked us off our feet,
everyone felt its inevitability rush through the eaves.
The air, not as it once was, threatened to harm us,
as though remade by some nefarious alchemy,
making each breath a risk.
Stranger, friend, family member, now stand-offish,
signs, masks, and suspicions exacerbate our fears,
and personal space takes on a lonely significance.

Neither hot nor cold, lukewarm

This fiery dragon consumes politicians' words,
and deflates puffed-up egos, setting fire to their verbiage.
Power changes so quickly when the world is ablaze.
Word ninjas cannot escape the inescapable truth
as they try to shake off core values they love to espouse.
It's the fiery one that exposes our misplaced faith,
our elegant, misplaced ideas dance wildly in its flames,
among the acrid smells of political bantering.

I know that my redeemer liveth

Noah's Ark floats on empty waters, full of strangers,
isolated but together.
A black dove flies wistfully over the silent waters.
She passes places of prayer, now abandoned,
hospitals full of supplicants, barely surviving.
Soaring above white suburbs, she weeps.
In city centres, she mourns the near-empty streets.
Nesting in an olive tree, musing over the virtue of returning,
she picks up a twig riddled with insects
and wonders if a drowned world will ever learn.

DESERT IN BLOOM

To Larry, who taught me how to love nature

The desert is no Wordsworthian country,
it's a far cry from any green and pleasant land,
but this forgotten Eden delights me with its strangeness.

Concealed from the unrelenting sun there are sleepers,
waiting,
full of hope, hiding in their natural dark womb
waiting for some dark cloud god to dance the rain
atop the dry encrusted wilderness,
hoping heaven will storm the barren earth
with a mighty wrath to flood this accursed paradise,
making noise enough to awaken those expectant sleepers
who dream of blooming in the world above.

And, though their time is short, I love to see them rise,
resplendent in beauty, crowned with a host of colours.

Glorious wildflowers gently soften the desolation,
chicory, poppies, forget-me-nots,
pincushions, dandelions, audacious in their fragility,
resourceful pragmatists, seducing pollinators,
star-kissed, moonlit, sun-drenched natural wonders,
fiercely stubborn in their determination to survive,
miraculously defying odds with indomitable strength.

MY SAN ANDREAS FAULT

My catastrophic thinking is anything but silent;
it comes in seismic existential shifts.
Each diminutive magnifies to great proportion,
ideas quake as once-held cherished beliefs
disassemble into utter chaos.
Inside this mind beats the heart of tomorrow,
teetering on a tectonic plate of human magnitudes,
shapeshifting between the familiar and unknown.
When the big one hits, this brain will release
a multitude of possible variables,
each of them believable at least for a moment.

Walking on the solidness of this illusion,
I know that underneath this surface
molten lava bubbles up.
Furious fiery waves crashing underfoot, unnoticed,
licking against the painful sores of my reality.

WHERE ANGELS FEAR TO MINISTER

Angels, stethoscopes haloed around necks,
stop to cover their faces.
Transformed by caring sterile lighting,
they're separated from human suffering.

Smiling, they saunter into the breach,
unprepared, fearing what is to come,
bolstered by applause and din of bin lids,
wondering if tonight they will occupy
a lonely place at the foot of the cross.

A host of virtual voices weep as they try to stare
down their isolation by singing.
Wary of the watchful ministry of angels,
they fear the caring medical pragmatism
of godly choices calculated by reason,
in which lives are measured on a scale of importance.

Angels skillfully cover their hearts.
Faced with inexplicable and impossible odds,
they know how easy it is to fall from grace
by a simple flip of a switch.

TEXTING EROS

I've always yearned for and desired love,
a seasoned passion, and something beyond
the showy rituals of coupling.
I had it for a brief spell, a blip in time,
but I'd never imagined us ever becoming word-weary,

silent...
                    sitting in a restaurant...
        apart,

divided by our digital distractions,
defining our privacy in singular terms.

Squandered now, those bold tender quips
that made me laugh,
swept aside by casual politeness,
courtship ridiculed in thoughtless civility,
favouring instead a lighter vacuous touch.

Glancing demurely, I envy the strong,
affectionate hold you have on your phone,
your eagerness to tap, scroll, swipe,
click your attention to somewhere else.

It's not as if we're unaware of petty discomforts,
they're impossible to avoid.
Now, retreating to our familiar comforts,
we hope for the virtual promise of release.

Sometimes, I edge a little closer,
readying myself to leap, only to fall back,
hiding behind the false intimacy of technology,
and the artifice of affection.

If only we could free ourselves from common courtesy,
dismantle our well-meaning boundaries,
restore our hearts to what they once were,
and risk all in a moment of abandonment,
diving headlong into the gaping mouth of longing.

FOSSILIZED GIANTS

I am among the last of the dinosaurs,
among the few to believe that all is not well.
This fragile life is near to becoming extinct.
Our profound naivety will catch us off guard,
and from the skies, our demise will fall upon us
as we sleep,
its musky poison leaching out into clean air.
We'll disappear under a meteoric shadow
to become the last of our species.

For too long we've dominated the Earth,
fearful creatures who have grown too big,
too arrogant to see our undoing in the heavens.
Soon, the brute truth will hit us with force,
polluting all that we breathe,
killing the grass beneath our feet,
until we become fossils of a lost opportunity.

WARNING TO WALL BUILDERS

Let's go down to Jericho and build a wall;
there we can listen to the sound of trumpets
in the distance,
watch as the troops circle our fortifications,
stare blindly at their eyes full of tomorrow,
laugh at their legs bruised with emboldened hope,
never suspecting that soon we'll be on our knees,
for not recognising the value of a good tune.

DARWIN'S ANGEL

The wings of pandemic isolation cover me.
Under its powerful expanse;
insidiousness makes me reimagine
who I am,
separates me from the reality I once knew.
This finite angel of death reduces and enlarges
the elasticity of my soul.

I am cognizant enough to know none of it matters.
If I bless or curse this messenger, nothing changes.
It exists, lives, and struggles to survive
regardless of what I think.

Our lungs cannot hold out forever,
prayer almost seems futile –
after all, this virus was created to be like us,
to live, evolve, and, if need be, kill,
so that it might continue.

SALVE REGINA

In memory of Dr. Lorna Breen

From the Home of The Ark's car park,
she texts her dad, (complete with a 😄).

49 years old and steadily sinking,
her world lies beyond the horizon of the news.
Once infected, she is now deemed a winner.

Returning to her station,
suffering no longer a mystery to her.
Death casually strolls behind her,
his cold breath immune to pity or mercy,
Death shows no bias, young or old;
all will drown in their secretions,
sometimes aided by her caring touch.

Sanitizing, sterilizing all human feelings,
she forces herself to look at the caged body,
suffocating.
Lights strobe, bleeping in futile regularity,
a heart stops, hers beats faster, she knows
chaos once admitted order be damned.

Somewhere a family sings heartfelt lamentations
softly into the silence.
Somewhere in isolation, their loved one
maybe a father, like her own,
has relinquished the final grip of hope,
his lonely breath stopped,
by the unseen enemy.

Vigorously, she scrubs the raw
dried-out flesh of her hands,
clean and free of contamination.
They are no longer the conduits of love,
but the stoic hands of a detached god.

Removing the rosary,
she scours the crucified one,
washes the lifeless nailed body,
watches as Christ's mercy and goodness
slips into a dirty drain.

Alone, in the quietness of a car park,
she feels a dark familiar presence
pushing her under for a third time.

A text from her father,
(complete with an 🕊)
goes unanswered.

BEHOLD THE CROSS

A deadpan Jesus stares down at the pious;
their shopping list of petitions, ready at hand,
pushed through rosaries and creased fingers.
The clacking of plastic beads,
teased out by finite whispers,
are collected in throats raw with desperation.

One believes the crucified one is weeping.
Other witnesses see the saviour bleeding pity.

Between requests, they stare intently
at the expressionless figure,
expectant, waiting for the sign,
a twitch in the veil of divine silence,
something to dull the lust for sympathy.

In the gentle stillness, throughout the ages,
innumerable Christs have dried and cracked,
wounding and scarring the life of this living planet.

Behold the true cross,
carved from the heart of a healthy tree,
its form, grotesquely twisted,
stripped bare, beaten, and nailed,
hangs high above moral scrutiny
for the good of all.

Oh God, forgive us for we know
what we do.

THE DEATH OF A SWAN

His fortune-telling stories were lazy, canny,
redundant as a stale fortune cookie.
Nervously flighty, she seeks his knowledge.
What new journeys lie ahead of her?
Timidly, her swan neck tilts towards him.
Vulnerable, she's charmed into intimacy.
Reading her palm, lined with possibilities,
he traces a faint hope into her desperation.
Balancing unsteadily on the verge of risk,
she ruffles her billowy feathers in anticipation
of a giddy, delirious flight into the unknown.

Switching gambit, his soft words smooth
out her noble troubled finite form.
Grooming her glorious white wings with praise,
he whispers assurances to silence her fears,
and a bluster of cheap phrases catches her up
into a sudden desire to climb lofty heights.

With a magnificent show of unfurled wing tips,
she surrenders to his elevated words
and her dreams begin to soar.

A fortnight passes by,
and our swan has fallen out of the skies.
Lungs, robbed of puff, wheezing with foul sickness,
she listlessly relinquishes all thoughts of tomorrow.
Her fortuitous wings, no longer flight-worthy,
lie within the confines of a machine.

Traced now by needles,
her lifeline is measured by science.

BEHIND THE DOOR PEOPLE

'I only speak to lonely people,' she says,
'hospitals are full of them.
People without a soul to care for them.'
Apparently, my case is not ranked among them,
since I'm bedded among a chorus of visitors,
my need falsely prioritized with a superficial glance.

As her volunteer heart saunters away,
I watch the gap widen between us,
nothing earth-splitting.
I'm one removed,
invisible to the naked eye, suffering only
the small lesions of petty impoliteness,
splitting over time, imperceptible
to those who can't see.

I speak for the lonely people.
sidestepped by subtle avoidances,
cheered on by blind assumptions,
visible only to the probing mind,
whose heart lies not on a sleeve,
whose voice is silenced by those
who feast upon the invisible worm
that thrives upon the crust of separation.

REQUIEM IN BLUE

For Derek Jarman

I want to write a poem,
something more than white or black,
celebrating the wonderful cerulean awning
that covers me.
Blue makes me happy not sad.

My spirit luxuriates in joyous aquamarine,
enthralled by its turquoise hope,
bobbing up and down in a blissful sea
of blue-ish contentment.

My world will surely end in blueness,
its final notes of azure cascading down
onto my ashen face wet with tears of teal.

Across a verdant pasture of delphiniums
a blue god dances towards me in indigo
while sapphire angels play their symphony
to the cacophonous beat of cobalt rain.

When his divinity manifests itself,
I am overcome by blueness,
my heart overflowing with blue delight,
and my uneasy consciousness
gratefully wanders after him,
upwards and onwards to rest on a bed of lapis lazuli.

DIVINE MISERY

A Song of Longing

Emily Dickinson buzzes around the place,
her mobile, set to vibrate, remains silent.
Moses touches his stony heart,
stuttering, he repeats her well-known phrases
as she plays with his hair.

He playfully admires the symmetry of her lines,
while she listens to him obsessively recite
each poetic quatrain.
Emily enjoys tying his thoughts into knots,
turning them into pretty bows.
Moses wonders if there is any mystery behind her form.

As Emily's tortured thoughts of love
spin around her heart's womb,
verses spill out of her head,
colliding with the force of two snails copulating,
minutely significant, epic in proportion.

Moses jibes, 'They'll love you for that one.'

Her virgin hands braid his sidelocks
with brute force.
Haunted by unfulfilled passion, barely formed,
she scolds the patriarch,
moving her hands gently across his bald pate.

'Look at us,' she quips,
'outsiders peeking in. Your fairy stories,
always teetering on the verge of the melodramatic.
Christ, what a bore!

And me a blathering Miriam
singing to these four walls,
dancing barefoot on the cross of desire,
exposing all of my cracked heart
that no one cares to see.
Pathetic is our pathos.'

Moses touches the braids,
they are the same yet different.
Tied so tight, rigid, and inflexible,
they righteously hurt him.

'Soon, maybe they'll text you.'

Kissing him lightly on the forehead, she sighs,

'And maybe one day you'll find your forever home.'

SPIRITS OF THE PAST

What beguiling nexus brings me back here?
Traipsing over the soul of Donegal,
navigating my way through clumps of heather,
mosses, lichen,
and the elegiac call of linnets.

My hand enters the dank moss, squelches,
pushes deeper into the mucky soil
so that bog juice oozes through fingers,
the coolness, comforting to an exile's heart.

A mélange of senses rouses my soul,
too deep for my understanding.

My gaze lingers over the Swilly,
below the ephemeral gaze of brooding eyes,
following me in my search,
their distinctive wispy contours
shifting in the clouds hovering above me.

As their grey shades cloud out the sun,
they whisper stories of untold suffering.
Exiled Earls, longing to return,
cleave to this place, refusing to be displaced.

Grianne and Diarmuid searching,
tormented by a hungry last look,
craving the taste of the other,
finding no pleasure among the heather.

Stick women, men and children
dead on their feet, hungering,

bowed down by this sorrowful sod,
return again and again
in the gale force tumultuous sighs.

Drenched in this fine mizzle,
steeps a noble sadness,
and a deep longing to return.

My bog soul houses an ancient race within,
mired in this place I call home,
yearning, like me, to be gathered in.

EL ROI

I met Hagar at the side of the road,
none too pleased with her ignominious lot.

'Love is felt most keenly in betrayal',
her laughter splintering into a crown of thorns.

'Never trust a God-fearing man.'

Hagar's toes sink into the dust as she etches
a crescent moon into the soul of the earth.

'There's no fool like an old fool.
Abraham lived by a long-standing covenant,
dreaming of stars, even naming them his own.
Taking me to himself, I believed in his dreams.
Until I became the line in the sand between nations,
with enough grit in my soul to aggravate even brothers,
finding myself caught between a rock and the stars.'

As she spoke, I saw Abraham through her eyes,
an old man who enjoyed playing chess with God,
complicating life's choices with vague schemes
so his rightful progeny might endure.

Caressing her magnificent belly, a world within worlds,
she shouts to the wind, '*El Roi*,
dirt, sand and stars are all the same.
Tomorrow, my dreams will grow in ways not conceived.
All of us are born from the sacred womb of God.'

STRANGE FIRE

A strange ignoble fire ignited in me.
Its rage, unchecked, untamed,
burning every good thought to ashes,
ancient columns fall to the ground,
for nothing good escapes such flames.

Arriving at Mr. Moses' house, I was still smouldering.
His eyes scrutinised me for a sign of life,
but all that was living had died in the fire,
only a ghostly residue remained,
the unfinished business of a spirit kind.

'You found us then. No fun getting up here.
Switchbacks up that mountain take it out of you.'

Aaron, a mangy cat, wouldn't stop meowing.
Crawling under my legs,
the lively feline showed no respect whatsoever
for the dearly departed.

'The missus made us some lovely cheese bread.
By the looks of you, you could use some nourishment.'

When my cold dead hand brushed against Aaron's collar,
his soul purred with a satisfied hymn of approval.
His constant preaching at me finally paid off.

A door opened to a waft of delicious smells.
Silhouetted, Mrs. Moses beckoned us to come.
Channelled by a generous smile, I quietly obeyed.

Amid the embers, a divine smell rose to greet me,
the lavish feast warmly enveloped my senses.
My hope, to my surprise, awakened, untouched by fire.
Mr. Moses blessed and broke the bread,
and a gentle sign of gratitude emanated from my lively
'Amen'.

EVERYONE LOVES A GOOD STORYTELLER

In the new revisionist era,
every retelling is completely trustworthy.

Isaac shoves the old curmudgeon God aside,
Abraham is laid upon the altar,
watching as his son sharpens the knife,
hoping it cuts deep enough to make
an everlasting impression.
Abraham is mistakenly naïve and gullible.

When the sea refuses to open,
Pharaoh trounces Moses and his illegals.
Miriam shakes her tambourine to the sky,
singing pretty songs to keep women
under the heels of men in perpetuity.

Raised on video games of giants and heroes,
David's avatar is no match for Goliath.
Slain and left for dead, David returns
to counting sheep and dreams
of making music to charm the ladies to his bed.

Satan takes the throne of heaven,
and we applaud, 'It's time for a change.'
The just are consigned to a fiery pit,
ventilated of hope, and sterilized
of love and compassion.

Sacred words no longer confuse and perplex us,
out of the humdrum of social media, a god rises,
a giant ego, a Lord of Lies
(commonplace variety).

BY A HAIR'S BREADTH

Samson needed a haircut

She had nothing to fear anymore,
she cuts his hair because he needs it.
There is no more Samson left in him.
His strongman years of wrecking temples
a thinning memory,
scantily thatched by age.

Baring his pink crumpled crown to her,
she sees no eyes in the back of his head,
the parchment skin pales insignificantly,
into his uneven noggin.

Exhaling,
abandoning her thoughts in a hair's breadth,
she touches his head, remembering,
the brute that branded her his own,
shaking the pillars of her being with a glance,
bending her will with the force of a god.

Her rage falls lightly onto the greying floor.

Tethered now by civility and maturity,
she hacks at the remnant of his power,
their intimacy curdles in her stomach,
as she fights the urge to sink the blade
into a godly artery.

He had made her weak,
unprepared for those who came after,
those who captured her vulnerability
with the detached look of Vermeer,

studying her movements and form,
disregarding the open soul before them,
dispassionately, stroking her beauty to satisfaction,
objectifying naivety with the fascination of a voyeur.

Watching her reflection,
she alone sees the hidden scars.

What they would think of her now?
A weathered doll poised over a decrepit man,
still craving his affection,
cutting into the past with detached abandon,
Vermeering herself.

Watching as she clips,
he sees the blade come perilously close.

WINTER IN THE DESERT

Loneliness is written all over their faces,
refusing to be exorcised.
They speak of aloneness, peaceful solitude,
a foreign concept to my frantic mind.
A world rages inside my head, *news, news, news,*
an angry mob of hostile voices muscling in,
robbing me blind of every quiet moment.

Here in the winter sun, a desert surrounds me.
Its gentle season warms memories of bitter cold,
of incessant inclemency, forcing its way through crevices,
with bone-chilling drafts,
and my necessary confinement to the hearth,
thoughts in a state of perpetual freeze and thaw,
longing to find solace in the warmth of another like me,
alone.

Fear not the solitude,
a refrain to trigger an alarm in any sensible person.
Solitude and I have always eyed each other from a safe distance,
measuring the possibilities of an amiable connection,
or speculating if the chaos and silence can ever reach a lasting truce.

TRIGGER HAPPY

Don't play with matches,
look both ways,
take my hand, and don't run off,
you'll understand *why* someday,
say please and thank you,
play nice.

With morning cautions prayerfully tendered,
messy dishes are assigned to the sink,
and small legs run towards a future
alive with expectation and hope.

Order is restored safely to a quiet house,
dishes cleaned, the excited chaos tamed,
and returned to a semblance of stability,
where everything feels right with the world.

Or is it?

In minutes, 19 small bodies explode,
futures fall in a ring-a-ring o'roses.
Sirens, flashing lights, news broadcasts,
forcefully rouse the sleepy day's tedium
into another, another, another, another,
another, a rubric of rueful awakenings,
with two more educators dispensed of
in the proud land of the happy trigger.

WHEN LOVE FALLS FROM THE STARS

For those who have and continue to be persecuted because of their sexual preference

When love fell from the stars,
he boldly strutted into my rigid Eden
where fondness is rare, desire exiled,
alienated from the pleasures of a sensuous moon
that lie beyond the pale refuge of touch.

His strong body fell from a place of beauty,
punished, no doubt, for consuming knowledge.
Refusing to conform or be controlled,
he was no longer a starry-eyed believer.

When love fell into my bed,
loneliness and I became strangers.
Love stretched the boundaries of my joy,
unbound my marriage to seclusion,
wedded me to dangerous cravings,
driving my sensual soul to desire
the consummation of forbidden fruit.

In the sultry waters of my imagination
false piety failed to suffocate the longing
loneliness kept afloat
till the day it found you in a tempest.
Your ethereal form, crudely shaped,
not as a devil or a god but as a man of erogenous virtue,
handsomely solid in stature.

Love, stay with me.
Your place is not among the stars.
It's here, dancing under an opulent moon,
soaking in the sweat of our hardened desire,
merging our bodies into Erin's dark sod,
until dawn greets us with its damp kiss.

THE ONE WHO ROCKS THE CRADLE

We're told God rocked the world to a lullaby
with nursery rhymes enough to make us sigh,
boughs were broken, babies fell into space,
tales to put us back into our rightful place.
Parents cannot be trusted to do what is right,
playing their not-so-subtle games of daring and might,
tempting us to bite the apple if we dare,
frightening us with ghoulish notions of punishment;
it's folly to believe in myths and storytelling,
religious fanaticism is nothing but compelling.

ROAD TO NOWHERE

We've come a long way from back there;
there, where we had nothing to call our own,
except for dignity and self-respect,
and it is that dignity brings us here,
here, where we refuse to be taken back there.

So, let us travel together somewhere,
somewhere that leads to love and not fear,
fear of the one who is different to us,
where difference is not recognised as hostile.

ONE STEP FORWARD, TWO BACK

I encountered my younger self today,
we seem to meet a lot in recent times,
sometimes we side-step each other politely,
dancing delicately around the other,
embarrassed by the prolonged gazes,
but always comforted and discomforted
by the lingering presence of the other.

He looks well, full of unwarranted hope,
with a glint of idealism fresh in his eyes.
How can I tell him it won't last?
When the heart's young, it rarely listens;
at least he smiles bravely at his old man,
tomorrow, sadness will blunt his spirit.

My fondness for the boy excuses his naivety,
his unfailing optimism forgives my cynicism.
I am as much a mystery to him as he is to me.
We, the continuum of a singularity,
are essentially the same timeless ageing riddle.

BLIND FAITH

You fed me honey,
sweetness to suckle me to ripeness,
nourishing my lust for you
with the promise of much more.
I smiled when you kissed me with snow,
watched as the thaw melted,
tearfully, into a cold vastness of unknowing.

When I fed you cherries, hardened by a cold moon,
you warmed them tenderly on your tongue,
but when I kissed you with sand
I saw you wince from the grit of knowing.

In that moment of uncertainty,
the secret dealings of my errant heart
were exposed,
the cruel sweetness of desire lay uncovered.
At that moment, I disfigured the shape of us
with the revenge of Medusa,
turning your heart into a pillar of stone.

Now, your cold stony glare
judges and acquits my every action
as sharply as the eye of God.
You rail against my cries for compassion,
calcify pleas for pity with petty resentment,
reducing me to become a beggar of mercy
hoping for the kindness that is born of blind faith.

REMEMBERING

Our star-lit memories lie among the ashes,
walked upon by strangers who know nothing
of what was.
Idly stepping on the remains of yesterday's romance,
they are unaware of the ghosts that linger here;
they insist on tugging at the centre of my gravity,
savagely dismantling what we once were,
until we return as empty as stardust.

I CANNOT TEAR IT ALL DOWN

I cannot tear it all down,
rip out the broken heart of it,
and be done with it.

I cannot stop the death-whisperer
from calling your names,
or stop the freezing melt

sadness from its gentle falling
into the grave of tearful sorrows.
I cannot shout it down,

force back the dimming darkness
that drowns out each light.
I've watched too many lights fade,

getting old, felt the particles of anguish,
waves of grief subside into resignation.
I've crept under the shadow of prayer,

sought the divine presence,
rested on the warm breast of faith,
until my tears faltered, and all hope grew cold.

I continue to linger in desperate waiting
for the waters to part ways,
and clear for me a pathway to promise.

ACKNOWLEDGEMENTS

I am indebted to so many people for their support, and these are only some of them: Larry, my other half, for his support; the minyan at JRC (Jewish Reconstructionist Synagogue) who continue to inspire me; Rev. Dr. Katie Miller for being a friend and my favourite talking head. My family, who have had their fair share of suffering and continue to endure, and The Black Spring Press Group for believing in my work and being willing to promote my efforts.

These poems have been published by the following:

'Six Feet Apart' and 'Footnotes' in *Irish American News*; 'Six Feet Apart' also in *Ritualwell.org*; 'The Cloud of Contentment' in *The Best of British and Irish Poets 2019–21* (The Black Spring Press Group).